BOOKS BY LUCY BOOTH MARTYN

THE FACE OF EARLY TORONTO
OSGOODE HALL
ARISTOCRATIC TORONTO
TORONTO:ONE HUNDRED YEARS OF GRANDEUR

FORTHCOMING

THE MAPPING OF VICTORIAN TORONTO [EDITOR]
WILLIAM JAMES & HIS CIRCLE
QUEEN'S PARK

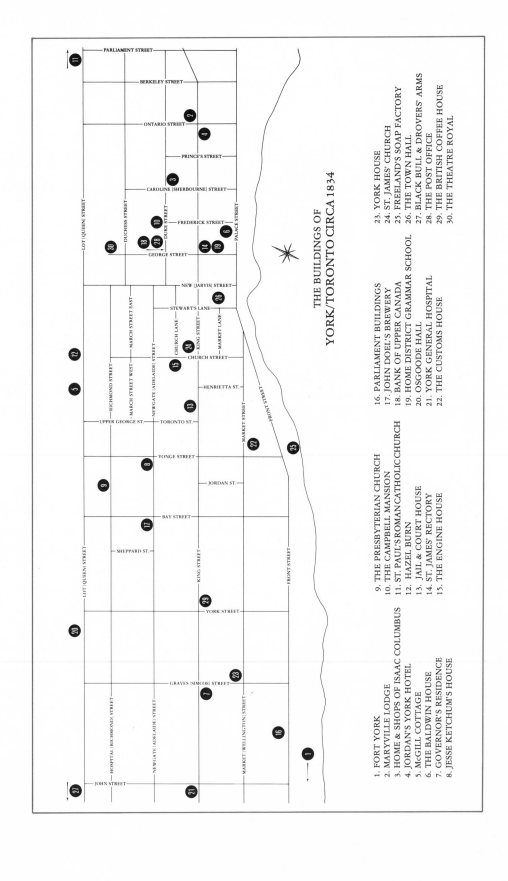

THE BUILDINGS OF
YORK/TORONTO CIRCA 1834

1. FORT YORK
2. MARYVILLE LODGE
3. HOME & SHOPS OF ISAAC COLUMBUS
4. JORDAN'S YORK HOTEL
5. McGILL COTTAGE
6. THE BALDWIN HOUSE
7. GOVERNOR'S RESIDENCE
8. JESSE KETCHUM'S HOUSE

9. THE PRESBYTERIAN CHURCH
10. THE CAMPBELL MANSION
11. ST. PAUL'S ROMAN CATHOLIC CHURCH
12. HAZEL BURN
13. JAIL & COURT HOUSE
14. ST. JAMES' RECTORY
15. THE ENGINE HOUSE

16. PARLIAMENT BUILDINGS
17. JOHN DOEL'S BREWERY
18. BANK OF UPPER CANADA
19. HOME DISTRICT GRAMMAR SCHOOL
20. OSGOODE HALL
21. YORK GENERAL HOSPITAL
22. THE CUSTOMS HOUSE

23. YORK HOUSE
24. ST. JAMES' CHURCH
25. FREELAND'S SOAP FACTORY
26. THE TOWN HALL
27. BLACK BULL & DROVERS' ARMS
28. THE POST OFFICE
29. THE BRITISH COFFEE HOUSE
30. THE THEATRE ROYAL

A VIEW OF

ORIGINAL TORONTO

THE FABRIC OF
YORK/TORONTO CIRCA 1834

LUCY BOOTH MARTYN

THE PAGET PRESS
SUTTON WEST & SANTA BARBARA

A VIEW OF ORIGINAL TORONTO

©

Copyright
1983
by
Lucy Booth Martyn

ACKNOWLEDGEMENT

Grateful acknowledgement is made to the staffs of
the Baldwin Room in the Metropolitan Toronto
Library, the City of Toronto Archives, the Public
Archives of Ontario, and the Public Archives of
Canada for their valuable assistance and suggestions
over the term of my research on this book, my
former books and the works in progress.

L.B.M.

ISBN-0-920348-30-0 (TRADE CLOTH EDITION)

FOR MY
GRANDCHILDREN
CAMILLE ALEXANDRA & MURDOCH ROSS

TABLE OF CONTENTS

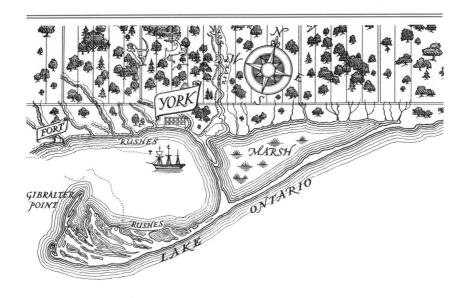

THE FABRIC OF YORK/TORONTO CIRCA 1834

FOR FORTY-ONE YEARS, THE TOWN OF YORK HAD BEEN THE CAPITAL of the province of Upper Canada, giving itself airs because of its importance in the raw country. Conceived in 1793 by Lt. Gov. John Graves Simcoe, who called it "our Royal Town of York", the town had no municipal government. York had no sidewalks (women wore wooden pattens to protect their shoes, because of the prevailing mud and filth), no sewers, streetlights, water supply, public transportation, garbage collection, and absolutely no plumbing. Roads were not paved; pigs rooted in the back streets in spite of a regulation that read: "Persons allowing their pigs to run about Town are liable to a fine of 10s.; if empounded, the poundkeeper's fee is 1s. and 1s.3d. per day for the pig's keep and after three days to be sold." There were no fire or police departments as we know them. It would, however, be unfair to criticize York's negative conditions too much, as most other towns of the day were no better. The population in 1833 was 6,094 and there were forty taverns and dram shops, heavily concentrated around St. James' Church and the Market.

In 1828, Anna Jameson in her *Winter Studies and Summer Rambles in Canada*, referred to Simcoe's "Royal Town of York", and its society, as being "fourth rate and half educated."

York's real problem was that there was no local government. There was no elected reeve or council to be responsible for town services, no officials who could be blamed for conditions, which nearly everyone deplored, and the root of the trouble was that there were no civic funds to remedy these conditions.

York was the seat of the Home District, a judicial and administrative unit which included the present counties of Ontario, York and Peel.

The district, as a whole, was administered by magistrates. They met in General Quarter Sessions of the Peace, at the court house. The magistrates were appointed by the lieutenant governor and held what little power of local government that existed, but they had very limited funds. York had no separate government except for the annual town meeting, which elected minor officials such as the town clerk, assessor, collector, pound keeper, town warden, and pathmasters.

It was an intolerable situation and was getting worse. Those who saw possible improvement realized it would mean increased taxation. The most radical elements among the Reformers, who were loudest in demands for various reforms, denounced the idea of incorporation for York, which would give a local government to the town. They declared it was a Tory plot to increase taxes, which would enrich the Tories.

Incorporation had been suggested several times. The benefits of self-government had been debated for years. (Montreal, older and bigger (pop. 40,000) had been incorporated in 1832.) Finally, when York's one and only member in the House of Assembly, William Botsford Jarvis, who was sheriff for the Home District, introduced the bill, it was passed with little opposition. The wordy document, [4 William IV c. 23] with ninety-seven clauses, became the Act of Incorporation on March 6, 1834, and York became a city, reverting to its original Indian name of Toronto. The name was unique and purely Canadian. It was the first incorporated city in the province. In fact, it was the first city.

In 1833, the Town of York was bounded by Peter, Queen, Duke and Front streets. In 1834, the City of Toronto was bounded by Bathurst, Dundas, Parliament streets and Lake Ontario. The city was divided into five wards (and "liberties") named after the patron saints of England, Ireland, Scotland and Wales, with the addition of St. Lawrence. Legislative power of the city was vested in the mayor, aldermen and common councillors in council. Each ward was to elect two aldermen, and two common councillors who would choose the mayor from amongst the aldermen. All male householders (owners or tenants) were entitled to vote for the council. In 1892 the "Saints", who had increased to thirteen, were retired and the wards were numbered, to a total of six. In 1859 the mayor was elected for the first time by the people and not by the council.

The 1834 election returns were:

WARD	ALDERMEN	COUNCILLORS
St. Andrew	Dr. Thos. Morrison John Harper	John Armstrong John Doel
St. David	William Lyon Mackenzie James Lesslie	Franklin Jackes Colin Drummond
St. George	Thomas Carfrae Jr. Edward Wright	John Craig George Gurnett

WARD	ALDERMEN	COUNCILLORS
St. Lawrence	George Monro George Duggan Sr. William Cawthra (replacing Duggan)	William Arthur L. Bostwick
St. Patrick	Dr. John Tims George T. Denison Sr.	Joseph Turton James Trotter

The first city council met April 3, 1934 with John Doel as the chairman. Of the elected members, twelve were Reformers, and by party vote William Lyon Mackenzie was elected mayor. The first appointed city clerk was James Hervey Price, the treasurer and chamberlain was Matthew Walton and the chief constable was William Higgins. The hoped-for Utopia was not automatically achieved by incorporation. During the first year the council spent a good deal of time bickering over old differences. Of course there were problems, and there was no precedent to guide them. They had inherited debts acquired by the Home District for the erection of public buildings, (£9000 to the Bank of Upper Canada) and as always, funds were very limited. It would take time for them to adjust, and regard themselves as a city council.

TORONTO'S COAT OF ARMS

There is a persistent legend concerning the origin of Toronto's coat of arms. Generations have believed that on a day in 1834, the new mayor entered a tavern on Market Lane, to discover a crowd gathered around an old soldier, who was making a chalk drawing on the floor. (Some say the artist was a sailor, whom Mackenzie had freed from jail.) In return for drinks and pennies, the man drew whatever customers requested. Mackenzie had been thinking of a design for the city's coat of arms, and asked the veteran to make a sketch. Paint and a thin sheet of metal were obtained, and with the mayor's prompting, a design was rendered. Mackenzie is reputed to have had a wood block made of this design, and commissioned the artist to paint the design on the back of his armchair in the council chamber. The original sheet of metal, is said to have hung for many years, over the bar of the inn, (which had moved to 36 Market Street), and was called the City Arms. It was believed that Mackenzie chose the motto: Industry Intelligence Integrity.

The 1834 coat of arms depicted a shield, supported by an Indian and Britannia— facing each other. The Indian held a tomahawk in his right hand, and a bow in his left. The shield displayed three lions in the first quarter; as in the Royal Arms of England, which the Lieutenant Governor had the right to fly, and which flew over Fort York. It was not realized, that Toronto had no right to use these royal symbols, and no one thought of asking permission of the College of Heralds in London, England. A beaver, a sheaf of wheat, and the steamship *Great Britain*, symbolizing the city's shipping interests, completed the shield. This coat of arms was never registered.

In the ensuing years the city used several different versions of this design. The supporters—the Indian and Britannia, were retained, but the original profile, changed to a frontal view. The design appearing on James Cane's 1842 map of Toronto, which was most often used on city documents, shows the Indian with two feathers in his headband, and a war club in his right hand. A variation, shows him with a bow in his right hand and a quiver of arrows over his left shoulder.

By 1961, it was realized that the Indian in the 1834 coat of arms, with his long feather headdress, was a Plains Indian Chief from the west, whereas the Mississauga Indians, who sold the 250,000 acres, including the site of Toronto, wore a different headband and carried different weapons. The beaver in the shield was redundant and was replaced by the white rose of York, the sheaf of wheat became a cogwheel, representing industry. The College of Arms viewed the steamship, as not being a proper heraldic design, but Toronto refused their suggestion of a classical galleon, as a suitable replacement. The old *Great Britain*, slightly altered, was retained. At the centre of the revised shield is the maple leaf, to which Toronto lays a special claim. In 1860 when the Prince of Wales visited Toronto, the maple leaf was worn by Canadians for the first time, in a parade on King Street.

Special dispensation from Her Majesty Queen Elizabeth II in 1961, enabled the continued use of the device of the Royal Arms of England, in the first quarter of the shield. Letters Patent were granted by the College of Arms on December 28, 1961, for a redesigned coat of arms.

THE GREAT SEAL OF TORONTO

The delightful legend of the old soldier drawing the city's first coat of arms on a bar room floor, is now largely discredited. No doubt, Mayor Mackenzie did refresh himself at a nearby tavern, and it is very probable that on some occassion an itinerant artist was earning drinks and pennies by amusing the customers, but there is no actual evidence that the coat of arms developed from such an encounter. This apocryphal story probably got its early publicity in Lyman Jackes', *Tales of North Toronto* [Vol. II], and it was later dicussed in Edwin C. Guillet's *Toronto Illustrated* of 1939.

It is now believed by many historians, as clearly stated by City Archivist, A.R.H. Woadden, in a speech to the Toronto Coin Club on August 25th 1962, that the Great Seal of Toronto preceded the civic coat of arms and formed a basis for its design. A municipality requires a seal for all legal documents, and as be the case, Toronto city council's minutes record that a committee was formed on April 8, 1834, to prepare the design for such a seal. The committee was composed of George Gurnett, (councilman for St. George's ward, editor and proprietor of the *Courier of Upper Canada*, a Tory who became Mayor of Toronto on four occasions.) John Doel (councilman for St. Andrew's ward, brewer and Reformer), and John Craig (councilman for St. George's ward, listed as "portrait, fancy and house painter"). Craig was the only one, of the three, with any artistic background, and it is unlikely that any of the group had knowledge of heraldic principles. Probably Mackenzie, who was widely read, knew more about the rules of heraldry than the committee, and no doubt he had the decisive word on the final design.

The council on April 23, 1834 authorized the mayor to use, as a temporary measure, "such seal as he saw fit", to legalize city documents. The seal was first used on May 10, 1834 when its imprint was affixed to By-Law Number One: "An act for the preventing and extinguishing of fires." The committee's final report was adopted on June 17, 1834, and a commission to execute the work was given to William Connell, tinsmith and engraver at 182 King Street. He was required to produce a finished seal and sketches for a coat of arms. The original cash book for the city shows several entries in the "City Seal Account". October 2, 1834 shows a payment of £10 for the seal, and November 22, 1834 records a payment of £5 for two sketches.

T. A. Reed, historian of early Toronto, wrote in *The Telegram* on April 13, 1954 that Robert C. Todd, a well known heraldic painter had at some earlier date made a large painting of the city's coat of arms, which the city council acquired in December of 1874. At that time it was related that the shield and supporters were designed by John Craig, the beaver was added by John Doel, and the motto by George Gurnett.

The seal and the first coat of arms are very similar, except the seal bears the motto on a scroll with the words in an alternate order. Neither the seal nor the original coat of arms was registered in the College of Arms.

STREET NAMES IN YORK

Colonel Simcoe was a dedicated royalist—enjoying the giving of names to places in his new province and to streets in his new capital. Musical Indian names of rivers and settlements were ruthlessly changed to familiar English place names, and the principal streets of York, were named in honour of the royal family. George III and his consort, Charlotte (with thirteen children), were generous in providing sources for names. Simcoe named the lakeshore road, (the main street in York) King Street, as was right and proper, but he failed to name a street, Queen. Perhaps he felt Charlotte had been sufficiently honoured in Prince Edward Island. George Street, (the original western boundary of York) was named for the Prince of Wales, and Frederick and York streets, were for number two son. Duke and Duchess streets, represented the Yorks. Since the duchess' name was Frederica, it would have been too confusing to name a street for her. Simcoe then lumped the remaining royal dukes, William [Clarence], Edward [Kent], Ernest [Cumberland], Angustus [Sussex], and Adolphus [Cambridge], in a street called Princes, which almost immediately was referred to as "Princess" Street.

The only royal female, to be honoured by Simcoe, turned out to be a disappointment. Caroline, princess of Wales, was the daughter of the king's sister Augusta, duchess of Brunswick. A street was named in honour of Caroline, but she behaved in such a bizarre manner—as if imitating her disreputable brothers-in-law—that her street name was changed to Sherborne, after Thomas Gibbs Ridout's home, located on that street. (The 'u' slipped in later.) King George IV removed his wife's name [Caroline] from the prayer book and refused to let her be crowned with him. The least that loyal Yorkers could do, was to remove her name from their street. However, she does live on in the name, Brunswick Avenue. As for the daughters of King George III, Simcoe honoured them when he named the townships. He commemorated the entire royal family with the townships of Charlottenburg, Charlotteville, Georgina, Adolphustown, Alfred (who died at the age of two years), Ameliasburgh, Augusta, Edwardsburgh, Elizabethtown, Ernestown, Fredericsburgh, Sophiasburg, and Williamsburgh—to cite a few.

When William became king in 1830, a street was named Clarence and his wife, Queen Adelaide, had a street named in her honour as well. Toronto eventually named a street, Queen in 1840 and then a Victoria, an Albert and an Arthur streets were named.

STREET NAMES

PRESENT	FORMER
Adelaide Street east	Duke Street
Adelaide Street west	Newgate Street
Bathurst Street north of Queen	Crookshank Lane
Bay Street south of Queen	Bear Street
Bay Street between Queen & College	Terauley
Bay Street north of College	St. Vincent
Bay Street south of Bloor	North Street
Berkeley Street (south end)	Parliament

PRESENT	FORMER
Broadview north of Queen	Don Mills Road
Broadview south of Queen	Scadding Street
Caroline Street (north end)	Allan's Lane
Chestnut Street	Sayre Street
Colborne Street	Market Lane
Duchess (1797 one block north)	Duchess (1793)
Duke Street	Duchess Street (1793)
Dundas Street east	Wilton Avenue
Dundas Street west	Agnes Avenue
Dundas west of McCaul	St. Patrick
Dundas west of Bathurst	Arthur Street
Front east of Market	King then Palace Street
Front, Bathurst to Spadina	Ontario Terrace
Jarvis south of Queen	New then Nelson Street
King Street	Duke then Palace Street
Lombard Street	March then Stanley Street
Market Street	West Market Street
McCaul Street	Renfrew Street
Parliament Street	southern Berkeley Street
Queen	Dundas then Lot then [in the west] Sydenham
Queen, east of Don River	Kingston Road
Queen, west of Spadina	Egremont Street
Richmond Street	Hospital Street
Richmond west of Spadina	Simcoe
Richmond east of Jarvis	Duchess
Sherbourne Street	Caroline Street
Simcoe Street	Graves Street
Soho Street	Maria Street
Spadina Ave. south of Queen	Brock
University	Park & College Ave. [as parallel streets]
Victoria Street	Upper George & Leader Lane
Wellington Street	Market Street
William Street	Dummer Street

Yonge Street [Young], planned as a military road by Colonel Simcoe, was opened by the Queen's Rangers to Holland Landing in the north, and did not extend south of Queen Street until 1818. It presently runs northward from Lake Ontario to virtual infinity— the longest street in the world. It acts as the watershed of Toronto streets. Those flowing east and west from Yonge street are numbered in these directions respectively, Yonge Street acting as the "main street". This was not always the case—in the early days, King street numbered from Berkeley Street. In 1833 some portions of streets remained without numbers and it had as yet to be established, that even numbering would be found on the north sides of streets and odd numbering on the south.

There are no photographs available of York taken circa 1834. Thus for our research purposes we must rely on two groups of documents. The first being contemporary sketches, and the second being drawings made from memory, or from contemporary written descriptions.

Those of the first group, small in number, are valuable as they are unique, but frequently they are not absolutely trustworthy. The definitive specimen being an 1835 D'Almaine portrait *John George Howard Surveying the Harbour*. This picture shows a series of buildings in the background, which have been attributed to Howard's hand. It has been generally known, over the years that Howard painted in the background—being his design for Government House—which he was never allowed to build. Actually, the buildings appear to resemble, much more closely, James Chewett's design for the Parliament Buildings (which were completed ca 1832, without the portico). Howard's design for Government House shows a six columned portico, flat roof and adjoining wings. The building in the D'Almaine portrait shows a structure with a four columned portico, detached wings and a mansard style roof. These are the most striking differences. Closer inspection brings forth more differences in design to support the possibility that the buildings are not Government House as planned by Howard, but the Parliament Buildings (with portico), as designed by Chewett.

Indeed it is most probable, that after John G. Howard was appointed as Toronto's first surveyor by Mayor William Lyon Mackenzie in 1834, a portrait resulted. D'Almaine in this portrait shows the Parliament Buildings as a suitable backdrop, they being the most prominent buildings on Front Street, overlooking the harbour. As the Parliament Buildings were constructed without the portico, D'Almaine would presumably have rendered them as such. Howard feeling the aesthetic need for a portico, and perhaps knowing full well of Chewett's desire to have a four columned design, either added the portico, with his own hand or, instructed D'Almaine to do so. Whatever the chronology of events, these additions to buildings can be most misleading.

VIEW OF THE PARLIAMENT BUILDINGS 1830/OWEN STAPLES [ca1889]

JOHN GEORGE HOWARD SURVEYING THE HARBOUR/D'ALMAINE 1834

DESIGN FOR A GOVERNMENT HOUSE/JOHN G. HOWARD/1833

[17]

A VIEW OF KING STREET FROM THE WEST/THOMAS YOUNG/1835

Similarly, Thomas Young's 1835 engraving *A View of King Street from the West*, (which became a well known Currier colour print) shows a tower and spire on St. James' Church, which had not been added, when the church was destroyed by fire in 1839. This idealized view, depicts King Street as being incredibly neat and clean, and altogether charming —most probably quite unlike the actual scene.

In a great many cases there are no contemporary pictures available. Nevertheless, we are fortunate to have numerous drawings, many of which appeared in the six volumes of Robertson's, *Landmarks of Toronto* from 1894 to 1914. John Ross Robertson, editor of the *Evening Telegram*, began a series of columns on Toronto history in 1888. He collected every illustration he could possibly find, interviewed hundreds of longtime residents, and engaged professional illustrators to make drawings of the early buildings thus described. These pictures, while undoubtedly better than none at all, are not always faithful renditions. It is difficult to remember exact details of roof pitch, gables, windows and chimneys, especially after some forty to fifty years. When the narrator was hazy about detail, the illustrator had to fill in as he assumed they must have appeared. Also, the illustrators may have been attempting to sketch a building as it appeared in 1830, when the narrator was describing a much later period of construction—with their information perhaps being based on information derived from the accounts of others. Accounts differed—one might insist that gables were east and west, while another remembered them to be north and south!

The *Telegram* series, invaluable as they are, contain errors which have been exposed and corrected by contemporary research. At times the account in one volume of the *Landmarks* will conflict with that of another. The *Landmarks* relies heavily on Reverend Henry Scadding, (rector of Holy Trinity Church) and his *Toronto of Old* of 1873. Robertson quotes pages of this work verbatim, without acknowledging Scadding. Scadding's work was not illustrated, though the author, like Homer, sometimes nods. We would have little published information concerning early York without him. Scadding who came to York in 1821, made pen & ink drawings of many of the earliest buildings, many of which are dated 1888—when the first *Landmarks* columns appeared— though many may have been drawn earlier.

The drawings which depict buildings from contemporary accounts are the most reliable, though at times lack detail. Architects are able to reconstruct the appearance of a building, working from early designs which have survived. A number of architectural views are extant. The Baldwin Room at the Metropolitan Toronto Library holds two major collections, those of Henry Langley and John George Howard. The Langley archive holds documents post 1855 and the Howard archive, post 1833.

As you will observe in the following pages, many watercolours made from early drawings show foliage obscuring architectural detail. We do wonder if this was not deliberate, to hide uncertainties.

COLUMBUS HOME AND SHOP

CUSTOMS HOUSE

Occasionally we are confused when two artists illustrate the same building. We do not have a picture of Secretary William Jarvis' house as it was prior to his death in 1817, but we do have an 1888 drawing attributed to William J. Thomson of the house when it was the Isaac Columbus home and shop in 1824. The 1912 watercolour by Frederick V. Poole of the house when it was the third Customs House in 1828 appears quite different. The house at the southeast corner of Duke and Caroline streets [Adelaide and Sherbourne] has a handsome front door and pleasantly symmetrical windows in the Poole picture, while Thomson's shows the other side and end of the house. Thomson also shows a later addition, which, because of the location of the house, appears to be on the incorrect end. Such discrepancies are most puzzling.

Similarly, there are two views of the Jesse Ketchum house. One shows the overpowering cubic tower, the other shows a view of Yonge Street looking west at Adelaide Street. This street view reveals a modest turret or belvedere, open with protective railing and a weather vane. The house has a cottage roof with Palladian windows on two levels, and appears to front on Adelaide Street. Once again curious comparisons.

THE KETCHUM HOUSE WITH CUBIC TOWER

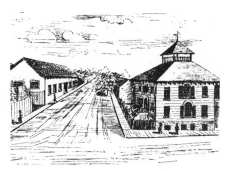
THE KETCHUM HOUSE WITH MODEST TURRET

One must remember that in the transformation from sketch to architectural view, to actual plans, and then through the period of construction, much can be altered. In the same vein, in the transcription of narration to sketch, and on through time departed, many a distortion may be rendered. Only with the advent of photography can we assure actual architectural confirmation.

A PLAN OF YORK IN 1793 from the Aitkens Survey (City of Toronto Archives)
TORONTO'S COATS OF ARMS (City of Toronto Archives)
VIEW OF THE PARLIAMENT BUILDINGS 1830 from a pen & ink attributed to Owen Staples ca 1889. (Metropolitan Toronto Library)
JOHN GEORGE HOWARD SURVEYING THE HARBOUR from a painting by D'Almaine of 1834. (Metropolitan Toronto Library)
DESIGN FOR A GOVERNMENT HOUSE from a photograph of the original watercolour and ink of 1833 by John G. Howard in the Toronto Historical Board Collection. (City of Toronto Archives)
A VIEW OF KING STREET FROM THE WEST from a Currier lithograph by Thomas Young 1835. (Metropolitan Toronto Library)
COLUMBUS HOME AND SHOP from a pen & ink attributed to William J. Thomson ca 1888. (Metropolitan Toronto Library)
CUSTOMS HOUSE from a watercolour by Frederick V. Poole after a drawing by Owen Staples ca 1888. (Metropolitan Toronto Library)
KETCHUM HOUSE WITH CUBIC TOWER from a watercolour attributed to F. V. Poole ca 1912. (Metropolitan Toronto Library)
KETCHUM HOUSE WITH MODEST TURRET from a drawing, artist unrecorded, ca 1889. (Archives of Ontario)

THE BUILDINGS

VIEWING THE FABRIC OF
YORK/TORONTO CIRCA 1834

FORT YORK 1793

THE QUEEN'S RANGERS, COMMANDED BY COL. JOHN GRAVES SIMCOE, served with distinction in the American Revolutionary War. They were disbanded in 1783 and reraised by Simcoe when he became Lieutenant Governor of Upper Canada in 1791. He did not trust the Americans, and he wanted a strong fort. When he founded York as his capital in 1793, he chose a site opposite the only entrance to the harbour. It was beside a creek, slightly west of modern Bathurst Street, at the edge of the lake. With Lt. Robert Pilkington of the Royal Engineers, Colonel Simcoe planned stone barracks and earthworks to cover the harbour mouth. Lord Dorchester, the Governor General, vetoed his plans and refused financial support. Simcoe could only begin a blockhouse and set up a camp of thirty round log huts, erected by the Queen's Rangers under Capt. Aeneas Shaw. The huts were joined together by a palisade, and a few old condemned guns were acquired.

Peter Russell, the Administrator after Simcoe left in 1796, feared the Indians, and completed the two-storey log blockhouse on the east side of Garrison Creek. About eighty log buildings, within a stockade, housed the troops and their families. Major General Sir Isaac Brock, who became Administrator in 1812, said York was entirely open to attack, and began strengthening its defenses by erecting a temporary magazine. He planned new barracks and storehouses, but the Americans declared war before his fortifications were complete, except for two new works west of the garrison. Britain, standing alone against Napoleon, could spare little help. The gallant Brock captured Detroit, but was killed in October 1812 during the capture of Queenston Heights. The Americans wanted to liberate the poor Canadians (and annex their country). When York was attacked in April 1813 by a force of 1800 selected men, it was commanded by Maj. General R.H. Sheaffe.

He had 700 men, composed of a corps of Glengarry Fencibles, 50 men of the Newfoundland Regiment, about 100 King's Royal Regiment (8th), 350 from the 3rd York Militia under Col. William Chewett and Maj. William Allan, and 100 loyal Indians under Maj. James Givins. The defenders made a gallant resistance, in their makeshift fort, but were overwhelmed. Sheaffe ordered the fort's gunpowder magazine blown up, which killed and wounded some defenders, and killed the American General Pike and about two hundred other Americans, ending the Battle of York. The invaders had destroyed the Officers' Quarters and the fort's blockhouse, and the one at the Don. In the town the Parliament Buildings were burnt, and all contents destroyed. The Royal Standard, which flew over the fort, and the Speaker's Mace, from the Parliament Buildings, were carried off. The church and some private property were looted. Dr. Strachan's forceful arguments to General Dearborn saved York from utter destruction.

By November two new blockhouses, and a new Western Battery with four cannons were completed. By 1816 Fort York was in better shape than it had ever been, with guns mounted on traversing carriages. In 1841 a new fort (later called Stanley Barracks) was built at the Western Battery, and the old fort deteriorated. In 1861 the Americans were again threatening, and the old fort's ruined ramparts were rebuilt with two, thirty-two pounders mounted at the south side.

Historic Fort York is now a military museum, with eight early restored buildings, and open hearth cooking in the Officers' Mess, once the centre of York's social life. The Fort is manned by a Guard in the 1813 uniform of the 8th King's Regiment of Foot, and the Battle of York is graphically illustrated with films and dioramas. The brave Queen's Rangers are perpetuated by the Queen's York Rangers, a militia regiment with quarters in the Fort York Armoury.

FORT YORK from a watercolour attributed to Owen Staples ca 1912. (Metropolitan Toronto Library)

MARYVILLE LODGE 1794-ca1854

ONE OF THE EARLIEST HOUSES IN YORK WAS MARYVILLE LODGE, the handsome home of the Hon. David W. Smith (1764-1837), near the northeast corner of King and Ontario streets. It was a frame building, painted yellow, and designed by William Chewett, Deputy Surveyor. The house had some claim to elegance, and the grounds, extending north to Queen Street, were laid out with unexpected formality in the brand new town.

Maryville Lodge faced Ontario Street, set well back from the street line. A wide central hall opened to a large office on the left, which contained a fireplace, and a separate entrance from the street and to a porter's lodge at the rear. Behind the office was a spacious parlour which was used for dining. It was handy to the kitchen, which was in a separate wing in the rear, connected to the house by a passage. Opposite the office was the drawing room, with a bay window looking out to King Street. Behind this room was a bedroom and study. There were four bedrooms and a housekeeper's room upstairs.

Smith, who came to York with Governor Simcoe, was Acting Surveyor General (1792-1800), when he became Surveyor General. His name is found on many early maps and plans. On two maps of York in 1794 he showed Maryville Lodge, though letters to him from Chewett in 1796 speak of the house as unfinished, because of the difficulties of getting material and labour.

D.W. Smith, Executive Councillor and Speaker of the Assembly, was a colonel in the York Militia which he organized in 1798. He received part of his pay in land and acquired 20,000 acres, not readily saleable. At the request of Colonel Simcoe he wrote *A Short Topographical Description of His Majesty's Province of Upper Canada in North America* to which is annexed a *Provincial Gazetteer*. This work was published both in

1799 and 1813, and is valuable because it gives the original Indian, French and English names of many places now known by different names.

The property was almost self sufficient. Along the King Street side in the rear were stables for horses and sheep and a poultry yard. There was an entrance to a lane which led to the coach house, which had sections on one side for servants and chickens. On the other side were a mill, pig pen, wash house, blacksmith's forge and pigeon cote. Chewett planned the entire complex.

Smith returned to England in 1804 and was knighted. Thomas Stoyell, a non-practising doctor, lived in the house for a time— then the "Yellow House" became a small private school, kept by Mr. Judd and then by Mr. Castle, who locked unruly boys in the building with the cupola. In 1829 the house and twelve acres were valued at £1200. Mrs. Ross had a small school there in 1833. The house was demolished about 1854.

MARYVILLE LODGE from a watercolour attributed to Frederick V. Poole, date unrecorded. (Metropolitan Toronto Library)

HOME AND SHOPS OF ISAAC COLUMBUS 1798

WILLIAM JARVIS, PROVINCIAL SECRETARY AND REGISTRAR, BUILT HIS home on two lots at the southeast corner of Duke and Caroline streets in 1798. William Smith, who had erected Castle Frank for Governor Simcoe, was the builder. The house was one of the largest buildings in York. It was of squared logs cut on the spot, covered by white painted clapboard. It was 31 feet by 40 feet, with two storeys and an attic, with the main entrance on Caroline [Sherbourne] Street. The Registry Office was in a large corner room with an entrance from Duke [Adelaide east] Street. A handsome winding staircase led to the drawing room above the office. Jarvis died in 1817 and the house was rented to a man named Lee, who opened an English Chop House and Billiard Room there. He built the addition along Caroline Street and rented part of the house to James Padfield, who opened a school. In 1824 Isaac Columbus (or Colombe), a talented Frenchman, bought the property. He was a cutler, blacksmith, locksmith and gunsmith who could make jewelry, guns, skates and false teeth and repair surveyors' instruments. He was also an elder in the first Roman Catholic Congregation. In 1828-29, the Customs House had temporary quarters in Columbus' house. Because of cholera deaths and a suicide, the house was believed to be haunted and was demolished in 1848.

THE HOME AND SHOPS OF ISAAC COLUMBUS from a pen & ink attributed to William J. Thomson ca 1888. (Metropolitan Toronto Library)

JORDAN'S YORK HOTEL 1801

ONE OF THE EARLIEST HOTELS IN YORK WAS JOHN JORDAN'S YORK Hotel, on the south side of King Street, west of Ontario Street. Opened in 1801, it was a storey-and-a-half frame structure, and was for years considered the best hotel in Upper Canada. With its steep roof and dormer windows, it could have been transplanted from Quebec. After the Americans burned the Parliament Buildings in 1813, the Legislature sat for one session in the small ballroom of the York Hotel. The earliest public dinners and fashionable assemblies were held there. The first stone pavement in York was laid in front of the York Hotel. Flat stones of irregular shape from the lakefront were used to make the rough footpath. In the 1820s the foundations gave way, and the building became dilapidated, although it still functioned as a hotel for some years.

JORDAN'S YORK HOTEL from a watercolour attributed to F.V. Poole ca 1912, probably based on a drawing by Henry Scadding. (Metropolitan Toronto Library)

McGILL COTTAGE 1803-1870

CAPT. JOHN McGILL'S 100 ACRE PARK LOT 7 EXTENDED FROM modern Queen to Bloor streets, between Bond and Mutual streets. McGill (1752-1834), who was born in Auckland, Scotland and served under Colonel Simcoe in the American Revolutionary War, settled in New Brunswick where he married Catharine Crookshank. They moved to Upper Canada in 1792, and he was made Commissary of Stores and Provisions. His duties were important and varied. In 1796 a warrant, signed by Simcoe, authorized McGill "to supply from the government stores such quantities of rum as may be required to the men (Queen's Rangers) employed on the wharf and canal at York." This was the pier being constructed at the garrison and at a navigable opening into Garrison Creek. There is a 1798 receipt made to McGill for nails, spikes, brads, linseed, white lead, pick axes and glass. He supplied carpenters and materials and directed the building of the Government (Parliament) Buildings being erected by Lt. William Pilkington. McGill was an Executive Councillor, and was granted a front town lot of one acre. He did not live in town as most other officials did, but on his suburban farm. His home, McGill Cottage and grounds at the south end of the forest, occupied a square later known as McGill Square, bounded by Queen, Bond, Shuter and Church streets. The large comfortable house was on the west side of Church Street. In 1805 he became Inspector General and Auditor General. During the American invasion of 1815, the ladies of York took refuge at McGill Cottage. His only child and his wife Catharine died in 1819. Two nephews, Peter and James McCutcheon, lived at McGill Cottage. Peter inherited the bulk of the estate when John McGill died, changing his name to McGill in accordance with the terms of the will. In 1870 McGill Cottage and its two acres of land was purchased from the McGill estate by the Wesleyan Methodists, who built the Metropolitan Church there. St. Michael's Roman Catholic Cathedral had been built on part of the McGill property to the north. North of the Cathedral, a street runs east from Yonge Street commemorating John McGill.

McGILL COTTAGE from an oil attributed to W. Bartram ca 1850. (Metropolitan Toronto Library)

THE BALDWIN HOUSE 1803-ca1855

WHEN DR. WILLIAM WARREN BALDWIN, BORN NEAR CORK, IRELAND, settled in York in 1802, he boarded with the William Willcocks family on Duke Street. Willcocks was mayor of Cork, and postmaster and magistrate of York. Patients were few and Baldwin opened a boys' school in the Willcocks house. The next year, when lawyers were scarce, he was one of a small group who obtained a licence to practice law, by proving to Chief Justice Allcock that they were sufficiently educated. Also in 1803 he married Phoebe, the second daughter of William and Phoebe Willcocks.

Willcocks built a house for them on a one acre lot he owned at the northwest corner of Frederick and Palace [Front] streets. It was a frame house of one-and-a-half storeys, of pleasing proportions, no doubt planned by Baldwin, who was an amateur architect. It faced Front Street, with a side entrance on Frederick. The front door was quite handsome with side lights, and the school probably occupied the front room to the right. There was also a water lot across the street on the Bay shore.

On May 12, 1804, the Baldwin School got a holiday to celebrate the birth of the master's son Robert, who would later become a great statesman and the Father of Responsible Government in Canada.

In 1807 the Baldwin family moved to a property bought from Hon. Peter Russell, Receiver General and first cousin of Phoebe's father. The new home was at the northeast corner of Front and Bay streets, where William would build a large brick mansion in 1835. The frame house on Front Street was rented, and when Willcocks died in 1813, he left it to his older daughter Maria, who sold it in 1819 for £500.

When William Lyon Mackenzie (1795-1861), bookseller and editor of *The Colonial Advocate*, moved to York from Queenston in 1824, he took over the corner property at Frederick and Front streets. Like merchants in York, the family lived in the rear and upstairs, while the ground floor housed the newspaper office, editorial room, printing press and bookstore. It must have been crowded with his mother Elizabeth, his wife Isabel Baxter, her mother, his illegitimate son James and a number of younger children, a servant and one or two apprentices living in the house. According to William Kilbourn in *The Firebrand*, the bookstore window displayed "unflattering portraits of the Lieutenant Governor and prominent members of St. James' Church being roasted by a red gentleman with a pitchfork."

When Mackenzie failed to get the job of King's Printer, his editorials attacking members of the "Family Compact" became increasingly libellous. In June 1826 the scurrilous accounts of their private lives became so outrageous, that a group of younger members of the vilified families broke into the *Advocate* office when Mackenzie was absent. They destroyed the press and type, carrying some of it across the road and dumping it into the Bay. Mackenzie, on the verge of bankruptcy, sued and won damages of £625 and was able to set up much better than before.

Shortly after this raid, Mackenzie moved to Church Street, and the property at Front and Frederick streets was bought by Joseph Cawthra (1759-1842). Joseph and his wife Mary Turnpenny came from Yorkshire to York in 1803 with three sons and one daughter. In 1806 he opened an Apothecary Shop at the corner of King and Caroline streets. From patent medicines, cutlery, tobacco, brandy, hats and shoes, he soon expanded into tea, sugar, coffee and all groceries. He became a wholesaler, supplying groceries to most of the stores in the province. Around 1827 or 1828, he moved to larger quarters in the former Baldwin house and added a large storehouse. With his wife and William, his youngest son, Joseph occupied the house until his death in 1842. During these years, no doubt, he made alterations and additions to the house and shop. His son John (1789-1851), had married Ann Wilson in 1821 and settled in Newmarket, but John's children spent part of their time with their grandparents. John's son, Henry lived there while he attended Upper Canada College. Joseph's son, William (1801-1880), inherited the business which he had worked hard to increase, but he discontinued it in 1843. Joseph's widow died in 1847 and William continued to occupy the house until 1849, when he married Sarah Crowther, and moved to Jarvis and Bloor streets. William became a wealthy and philanthropic capitalist, and in 1853 moved to the magnificent stone residence he built at the northeast corner of King and Bay streets. William and Sarah were childless.

Henry Cawthra, Joseph's grandson, lived in the Frederick Street house until about 1852, and not long afterwards fire destroyed the house. Boulton's 1858 Atlas shows vacant land at the northwest corner of Front and Frederick streets. The house, where a great statesman was born, where the first Mayor of Toronto, who had in 1838 invited American soldiers into Canada to help found a republic, lived briefly, and where an immense fortune was begun, had vanished.

THE BALDWIN HOUSE from an engraving ca 1879 after a sketch by Dr. Scadding. (Metropolitan Toronto Library)

GOVERNOR'S RESIDENCE 1815-1862

GOVERNMENT HOUSE IN YORK WAS CALLED THE GOVERNOR'S RESI-
dence. When Lieutenant Governor Peter Hunter's house near the fort
was destroyed in 1813, during the American invasion, the Government
bought Elmsley House, which stood in six acres at the southwest
corner of King and Simcoe streets. Built in 1799 by Chief Justice John
Elmsley, it was white painted stucco and frame, 49 by 38 feet, the walls
and partitions filled with bricks, and the roof covered with shingles and
tin. There were six rooms, and a garret with a kitchen below stairs.
When Elmsley became Chief Justice of Lower Canada in 1801, his
house was occupied by Alexander McDonell, Sheriff of the Home
District and Solicitor General Robert Isaac Gray. Justice Thorpe was a
tenant briefly and then the house was vacant. The Crown took it over,
and for five years the Executive Council had offices on the ground floor
and the Surveyor General used the upstairs. In 1814 the Government
bought the house from Mary, Elmsley's widow, for £4000 and repaired
it. When Lieutenant Governor Francis Gore moved in, Elmsley House
officially became the Governor's Residence. Henceforth, there was
always a sergeant's guard on duty and proper military etiquette was
observed. Although Sir Peregrine Maitland, Lieutenant Governor
(1818-28), preferred his retreat at Stamford, he laid out the grounds of
Government House very attractively and added a conservatory. The
next occupant, Sir John Colborne, said the expenses of Elmsley House
exceeded his salary, and in 1836 when Sir Francis Bond Head was sworn
in, he inherited debts of £1050 and still had to spend £1000 for horses,
carriage and liveries. The position was an honour but no sinecure. In
the 1837 Rebellion, Head had the windows blocked up with timber,

[33]

leaving loopholes. When he was replaced by Sir George Arthur in 1838, Head exclaimed "Thank God I am at last relieved." In that year John George Howard was commissioned to build a ballroom, 50 feet by 30 feet. About this time the outer walls were encased in brick. When Upper and Lower Canada were united in 1841 and the capital moved to Kingston, the House was closed. From 1847 to 1849 it was the temporary home of the Normal School. In 1860 Government House had its greatest glory when H.R.H. Edward, prince of Wales lived there for five hectic days. There was much expensive refurnishing and entertainment. It then reverted to government offices, which were vacated for army officers who had not quite settled in, when the building burned down in 1862. The site is now occupied by Roy Thompson Hall.

ELMSLEY HOUSE, THE GOVERNOR'S RESIDENCE from a pen & ink in Robertson's, *Landmarks of Toronto*. (Metropolitan Toronto Library)

JESSE KETCHUM'S HOUSE 1813-1839

JESSE KETCHUM (1782-1867) WAS BORN IN NEW YORK STATE, AND
came to York in 1799. His tannery at the southwest corner of Newgate
[Adelaide] and Yonge streets, stretched along the south side of
Adelaide almost to Bay Street, and down the west side of Yonge nearly
to King Street. He also owned the block bounded by modern Yonge,
Adelaide, Bay and Queen streets. His large frame house, painted white,
stood at the northwest corner of Yonge and Adelaide. The flat roof of
the large square turret was surrounded by a high railing and formed a
good observation post. Ketchum made a dry sidewalk in front of his
property by spreading a layer of tan bark. He was a Reformer and
represented York County during 1828-34. Ketchum made a great deal
of money selling leather to the government. He gave land and money
for Knox Church and manse, and other religious and educational
institutions on his land. In 1837 he donated land to open up Temperance
Street through his property, stipulating that alcohol should never be
sold on the street. About 1839 his house was demolished and the land
cut into lots.

JESSE KETCHUM'S HOUSE from a watercolour attributed to F.V. Poole ca 1912.
(Metropolitan Toronto Library)

THE PRESBYTERIAN CHURCH 1821-1847

THE REVEREND JAMES HARRIS (1793-1873), BORN IN BELFAST, AND A
licentiate of the Secessionist Presbyterian Church in Ireland, came to
York in 1820. There was no Presbyterian Church in York, and he began
organizing a congregation. Jesse Ketchum, who was generous to a
number of struggling churches, donated the block bounded by modern
Queen, Yonge, Richmond and Bay streets, and provided funds for the
building of a church and manse. The building, completed in 1821, was
known simply as the Presbyterian Church. It was of brick and located
on the north side of Richmond Street, about 50 feet back from the
street, and seated about 400. As in all Scottish churches, the pulpit was
the focus, rather than the altar. The pulpit at the north end was so tall
that the congregation could hardly see the minister. Harris preached to
large crowds—some men were of the Assembly, including William
Lyon Mackenzie, who constantly complained in his *Colonial Advocate*
of the tunes used for hymns and psalms. Most of the congregation were
Irish and American tradesmen and artisans whose political beliefs were
suspected by the "Family Compact." Harris married Fidelia Ketchum
(1808-1874), his benefactor's daughter, and a manse was built on the
east side of Bay Street in 1825 by Ketchum. When the Scottish Church
was disrupted in 1843, his congregation was joined by a group from St.
Andrew's Church, and the newly organized church took the name of
Knox Church. The building had been called The Scotch Church or The
Presbyterian Church. In 1844, Harris was retired on a pension and
moved to Jesse Ketchum's farm at Eglinton—he was succeeded by
Rev. Dr. Burns of Paisley, Scotland. During his eleven years at Knox,
the Church was enlarged by a frame addition at the front, used for

church meetings. In 1847 Knox Church was destroyed by fire and a new brick church with a handsome spire, was erected facing Queen Street. Simpson's store paid rent to Knox United Church for many years and now occupies the block.

THE PRESBYTERIAN CHURCH from an etching attributed to Owen Staples ca 1912, after a pen & ink ca 1889. (Metropolitan Toronto Library)

THE CAMPBELL MANSION 1822

WILLIAM CAMPBELL (1758-1834), BORN IN SCOTLAND, CAME TO YORK
as a judge in 1811. In 1822, he built his late neoclassical, red brick
house, on two acres of land on the north side of Duke Street [Adelaide
east], facing Frederick Street. It had an elliptical fanlight, handsome
panelling, curving staircase, basement kitchen, and a pet alligator in
the garden. Campbell was Chief Justice (1825-1829), and was knighted
on retirement. After his death, the house was for many years the home
of Hon. James Gordon. Then John Strathy, a barrister, was a tenant
until his death. By 1890 it was the only house in a commercial area. It
became a vinegar warehouse, then was sold to the Otis Fensom Elevator
Co., which installed an elevator from cellar to roof. The Capewell
Horse Nail Co. was there in 1910, followed by the Hobbs Glass Co.,
which covered the interior walls with glass, and then the Masco Electric
Co. filled it with equipment. Miraculously the façade was never altered.
The house was bought in 1962 by the Coutts Hallmark Co., who
planned to demolish it, but agreed to donate it to The Advocates'
Society, a group of heritage conscious lawyers, if they would remove it
in six weeks. This was not much time to find a site, prepare a
foundation, and plan a complicated move. Canada Life Insurance Co.
had a fine vacant site in front of their head office at the northwest
corner of Queen Street and University Avenue. They would donate the
site if the city would forego the taxes. The city agreed, and on Good

Friday morning, April 1, 1972, the 300 ton, 41 foot high house began its mile long journey. Traffic lights, signs, telephone poles and transit cables were removed, manhole corners were shored up, streetcars were re-routed; everyone co-operated. Scrivener Projects Ltd. put the house on dollies with fifty-six wheels, and two trucks in tandem pulled and winched it to its new site—the longest journey in the history of moving brick buildings. Enthusiastic crowds accompanied this survivor of early York. The Ontario Heritage Foundation gave the Advocates a grant for restoration, and the building was opened as a private club in 1974 by the Queen Mother Elizabeth.

SIR WILLIAM CAMPBELL'S MANSION from a pen & ink attributed to William J. Thomson 1888. (Metropolitan Toronto Library)

ST. PAUL'S ROMAN CATHOLIC CHURCH 1823-1904

ON MARCH 25, 1806, THE CROWN GRANTED LAND TO THE CATHOLICS
in York, for a chapel. It consisted of nine-tenths of an acre on the north
side of Duke Street [now Adelaide], east of George Street. The
congregation was organized in 1807, in the home of Dr. James
Glennon, and he and Hon. Alexander McDonell, Speaker of the House
of Assembly, and Laurent Quetton de St. George, merchant, were
made trustees. There were few Catholics in York at the time and there

[40]

was no priest. Occasional services were held in homes by priests travelling through. When James Bâby, Executive and Legislative Councillor, became Inspector General in 1815, he moved to York and became the driving force for a church. By 1818 there were about 200 Catholics in York, mostly south of King Street, west of the Don River. Whenever Rev. Alexander Macdonell visited York, he stayed in Bâby's house and said Mass in the diningroom, which had been converted to a chapel. During his 1821 visit, the building of a church was discussed and he left many of the details to Bâby to arrange.

In 1821 the trustees, whose chief was now Bâby, sold the Duke Street lot, which was too small for a church, rectory and cemetery, to Sir William Campbell for £265. With the proceeds, they bought ten acres on Lot [Queen] Street, east of modern Power Street, at £20 per acre, and in May a "bee" was held to clear part of the land. John Ewart was engaged to draw plans for the church, with Parkes, the contractor, as builder. St. Paul's Church was opened in 1824 and completed in 1826, and was the only Catholic parish between Kingston and Windsor.

The building was of red brick, 90 feet by 46 feet, facing Power Street, then called Chapel Street, a short distance south of Queen Street. The long sides, of lighter colored brick, worked in a diamond pattern by the bricklayer Thomas Bond, were much admired, though considered rather curious. In February 1824 the Honourable James Bâby, writing to Rev. Alexander Macdonell, who became Bishop of Kingston in 1826, said " . . . if the cost is great, the building is well worth it . . . it is the neatest building of the kind in Upper Canada . . . also the cheapest, with roof, steeple, neat gallery, beautiful arched ceiling with cornices in plaster of Paris." The spire was surmounted by a cock, which many Catholic churches then used. (About 1850 it was felt that the cock was unsuitable and it was replaced by a cross). Ewart's church had dignified Georgian proportions, but his lancet windows gave it a romantic Gothic air. It is interesting to compare St. Paul's with Ewart's later York churches: St. Andrew's (Church of Scotland) 1830, and St. James' (Church of England), which he rebuilt in 1839.

The Reverend James Crowley was the first resident priest of St. Paul's from 1824 to 1826, and the following year Rev. Angus Macdonell, nephew of the bishop, became pastor, and the church flourished. In 1828 Rev. William O'Grady, who had a church in Ireland, visited York and offered his services for a year. He was good at raising funds to pay the church debt, but he got deeply involved in local politics, in alliance with William Lyon Mackenzie. When he used the pulpit to preach radical ideas, Bishop Macdonell rebuked him, but Father O'Grady defied the episcopal warning and continued to preach sedition. The bishop deposed him for insubordination—the rebel priest refused to leave and locked himself inside the church. St. Paul's Church was then placed under a solemn interdict, and there was turmoil and unpleasant publicity. For several months in 1832 St. Paul's bell was silent, divine services were prohibited and no religious rites could be administered.

Bishop Macdonell, whose seat was at Kingston, had a house in York where he was a Legislative Councillor. The interdict was not against the congregation, and they were able to hear Mass, make confession, be married, or baptised at the bishop's house at the southwest corner of New and Duchess streets, now Jarvis and Richmond. At St. Paul's, O'Grady admitted his few followers by the back door, to rival services in the church. The bishop expelled him from the diocese and finally O'Grady, threatened by police, left the church and founded a radical newspaper, *The Correspondent*. Mackenzie's *Colonial Advocate* was merged with it in 1834. The interdict was lifted and in 1833, the Reverend W.P. McDonagh replaced Rev. O'Grady. St. Paul's was the only church in the province ever to be placed under an interdict.

By 1842 the parish had grown to 3000, and when Michael Power chose Toronto as the seat of his newly created Diocese of Western Ontario, St. Paul's became a cathedral and remained so until St. Michael's Cathedral was built. Right Reverend Michael Power, D.D. died of typhus, while caring for the Toronto victims in the terrible epidemic of 1847.

St. Paul's Church was immediately north of the House of Providence, which was erected in 1854. A rectory was built in 1860 beside the church. A splendid new stone church, north of the old brick St. Paul's, was begun in 1887. It is the only church in the Italian Renaissance style in Toronto, complete with campanile. It was designed by Joseph Conelly, R.C.A., in Papal Basilica form and dedicated in 1889. Its interior is famous for the beautiful ceiling paintings depicting the life of St. Paul.

The old brick church, with a chapel added to the east end, became the parish hall, but was demolished about 1904 to make room for a new rectory (which in its turn had to make way for the expressway ramps). The cornerstone of the new parish hall was laid in 1914.

ST. PAUL'S from an etching attributed to Owen Staples after his original pen & ink, date unrecorded. (Metropolitan Toronto Library)

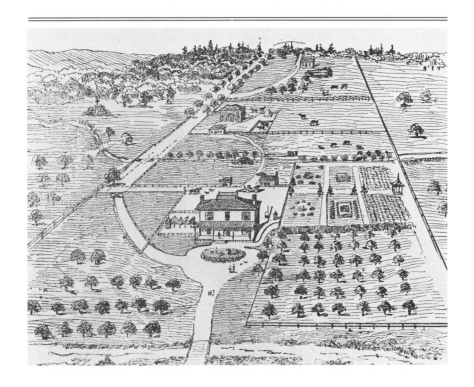

HAZEL BURN 1824-1847

JARVIS STREET RUNS THROUGH THE MIDDLE OF THE 100 ACRE PARK Lot 6 granted to Surveyor General David W. Smith. Provincial Secretary William Jarvis received the Crown grant of Lot 3, but in a three-way trade with John Small, Jarvis ended up with Lot 6, which extended from modern Queen to Bloor streets, between Mutual and George streets. Before he died in 1817, Secretary Jarvis gave the lot to his eldest son, Samuel Peters Jarvis (1792-1857), war veteran and lawyer. Samuel also inherited his father's tangled affairs, and spent years trying to untangle them and pay the debts. He is perhaps best remembered now, for his duel in 1817, with the eighteen-year-old war veteran and law student, John Ridout, son of the Surveyor General Thomas Ridout and brother of Thomas Gibbs Ridout. The two families seemed to be always opposed, and it is not clear what John said about the Secretary's debts, but Sam threw him out of his father's office. A few days later, when they met on the street, John attacked Sam. They were separated, but the encounter resulted in a duel. The excitable John fired at the count of "Two!" Sam waited for "Three, Fire!" and shot and killed John. He was arrested (his father died while he was in jail), but was later acquitted.

In 1818 Samuel married Mary Boyles, daughter of Chief Justice Powell, and soon began clearing the south half of his lot, which he called Hazel Burn because of the hazel nuts and the little stream. The house, completed in 1824, some way back from Queen Street, is believed to have been designed and built by John Ewart. It was a substantial brick building with a wide verandah and centre hall. Lawns, orchards and gardens were laid out, and in the rear were brick stables, a coach house, fowl house and rabbit warren. Samuel was one of the "genteel mob" who threw Mackenzie's press into the Bay in 1826. The editor had vilified all the officials, and implied that Sam was a murderer. In 1837 Sam raised and commanded a loyalist regiment, the Queen's Rangers. He was appointed Chief Superintendent of Indian Affairs, but was dismissed in 1845. In 1841 he sold a piece at the north end of his farm to St. Paul's Anglican Church.

By 1845 his inherited debts and his own difficulties led Sam to subdivide Hazel Burn. He sold a block, north of modern Carlton Street, (where the Canadian Broadcasting Corporation now stands),to John Ewart. John G. Howard, the architect-surveyor, was engaged to open up Jarvis Street (80 feet wide), and divide the land into lots. In 1847 the house Hazel Burn, standing in the way of the new street, was demolished. The black walnut woodwork was bought by Colonel Arthur Carthew, who put it in the house he was building on modern Lawton Boulevard. Shuter Street was extended through the site of Hazel Burn. The country lane, which was the mutual boundary between Hazel Burn and the McGill property, became known as Mutual Street. Several rooms in the rear of the house were left on the west side of Jarvis Street, and were converted into a house. The stables also remained on Jarvis Street for some years.

THE RESIDENCE OF COLONEL JARVIS from a pen & ink in Robertson's, *Landmarks of Toronto*. (Metropolitan Toronto Library)

[44]

JAIL AND COURT HOUSE OF THE HOME DISTRICT 1824

ON APRIL 24, 1824, LIEUTENANT GOVERNOR MAITLAND LAID THE cornerstones of the second jail and second court house in York. A procession of the Executive Council, judges, barristers, magistrates and principal citizens marched to the site on the north side of King Street between Toronto and Church streets, where the Governor and his suite waited. The two identical buildings of red brick, with cut stone trim, were designed by John Ewart and Dr. W. W. Baldwin. The contractor was John Hayden. The magistrates had to borrow £6000 to erect the buildings, whose gable ends with handsome pediments faced King Street at the south. They stood back about 100 feet from King Street, leaving a public space which was called Court House Square, where crowds gathered during elections, hangings, and other exciting occasions. Prof. Eric Arthur reports that this was the town's earliest attempt at "civic design." (Unfortunately this open space is now covered by buildings.) An underground tunnel joined the buildings. The jail on the west, completed in 1827, had a side entrance on Toronto Street. Its walls were forty inches thick, and there was a fifteen foot wooden fence around the rear and sides. Near the front entrance were the stocks for punishing petty offenders, and the gallows were set up in the jailyard in the rear for public hangings, which were a popular entertainment. The jail was crowded with criminals, debtors, lunatics and vagrants. In 1834 the Governor of the jail was Charles Barnhart. When the new jail was opened in 1840, the old one was used to house the insane, and was later incorporated in York Chambers.

The Court House, with a side entrance on Church Street, opened in 1826, and was used as a temporary Parliament Building from 1829 to

1832. The Legislature, whose buildings had burned down in 1824, because of a faulty chimney flue, had been meeting in the General Hospital. The 1837 rebels were tried and sentenced in this Court House, and Lount and Matthews were hanged in the jailyard.

The Quarter Sessions of the Peace of the Home District met in the Court House. The Home District Court, and the Police Office of the Home District were located in the Court House. The Court of Commissioners of Customs was held here. The Treasurer of the Home District, the Sheriff and the Clerk of the Peace also had offices there. When York became Toronto, the Home District Jail and Court House became the jail and court house of the city.

In 1852 a new court house was opened on Adelaide Street, and the old court house was rented as the City Theatre. For some years James Thomson had a dancing academy in the building.

JAIL & COURT HOUSE from a watercolour by John G. Howard 1835. [Jail to the left, court house to the right.] (Metropolitan Toronto Library)

ST. JAMES' RECTORY 1825-1902

THE REVEREND GEORGE O'KILL STUART (1776-1862), APPOINTED AS A missionary of the Society for the Propagation of the Gospel, was the first Anglican rector in York, from 1801 to 1811. His two-storey stone home, at the southeast corner of King and George streets, was the first rectory, and after 1807, a one-storey wing on his house acted as the first Home District Grammar School. In 1812 Rev. John Strachan, D.D., became rector of York, living in rented premises until his splendid home on the north side of Front Street, west of York Street, was completed in 1818. Dr. Strachan became archdeacon in 1825 and, when he became bishop of the newly created diocese of Toronto (which included all Upper Canada) in 1839, the St. James' Rectory became the Bishop's Palace. Strachan remained rector until 1847, when Rev. Henry J. Grasett became rector.

The beautifully proportioned red brick house on the south side of Adelaide Street, about 450 feet west of Jarvis Street, was said to be the third brick house in York, when it was erected in 1825. It was built by a man named Andrews, and it is believed that he intended it as a hotel. This theory is strengthened by the fact that when Rev. H.J. Grasett moved into the house, he found that every upstairs room had a number. He is listed in the 1836 Directory, as the "curate of the English Church." The house had been occupied by John Fenton, the eccentric first parish clerk, beadle and general factotum of St. James' Church, who was also clerk of the Police Office. Quite often, after announcing the hymn which he had selected, he would sing the whole of it with his own variations. When the rector would mount the pulpit above him, Fenton would lean back and cover his face with his handkerchief, until the sermon was over. Fenton was indispensable at St. James', and was also a class leader of the Wesleyan Methodists.

Grasett, who was appointed Bishop Strachan's examining and domestic chaplain and private secretary, occupied the house until his death in 1882. One can imagine the important conferences in the rectory, between the friends, bishop and rector. After the bishop's death, the rector became the first Dean of Toronto in 1867, and numerous distinguished clergymen made visits to the rectory.

The dean and Mrs. Grasett, nee Stewart, had a large family, and it is thought that not all the social events in the rectory were religiously oriented.

Before Canon Du Moulin's tenancy, the rectory was remodelled, and when he moved in 1886, the house was rented to the Children's Aid Society, as a shelter for destitute children. In 1902, during the cathedral's centenary celebrations, the old rectory was demolished and replaced by a more modern house on the same spot, dedicated by the bishop in June 1904. This was sold to the diocese in 1931 for synod offices, but was demolished when the present synod offices were built for the Anglican Congress of 1963.

ST. JAMES' RECTORY from a watercolour attributed to Owen Staples ca 1912, after a pen & ink attributed to W.J. Thomson ca 1893. (Metropolitan Toronto Library)

THE ENGINE HOUSE 1826

FIRE WAS A SERIOUS THREAT IN A TOWN WITH SO MANY WOODEN houses and open fireplaces, when the sole supply of water was from wells and the Bay. An early regulation in York required ladders to be attached to the roofs of all houses, and two leather or canvas two-gallon water buckets to be hung by the front door. A fine was levied if these were used for any other purpose. Regular chimney sweeping was also required. Early bucket brigades, when neighbours rallied round, were helpful but unorganized. In 1802 Governor Hunter gave an engine—a vertical pump on wheels, operated by teams of volunteers standing at each side. This first fire engine was part of the American loot in 1813, and is on display in a Washington museum. To encourage men to join the York Fire Company (the first engine company founded in 1826), members were granted exemption from military duty, jury duty and other town offices. The men, unpaid volunteers, elected Hugh Carfrae as their captain, and he was re-elected for the next six years. The first Engine House or Firemen's Hall was a two-storey brick building, erected in 1826 on the west side of Church Street, south of St. Andrew's Church between Court and Adelaide streets. There was a small bell tower in the rear. The bell rang the alarm, and was later given to St. James' Church and hung in the belfry. When the church burned in 1849, the old firebell was destroyed. There was a long shed in the rear of the firehall for drying the leather hose. (Later firehalls were distinguished by tall towers for drying the hose.) The Engine House became a club for the volunteers. In 1828 the York Fire Co. and the Alliance Fire Assurance Co. offered prizes of three, two, one and one-half dollars to the first four carters, who would bring barrels of water from the Bay. There was fierce rivalry among the carters, and the winners jolted their loads so much that they often arrived at the fire with very little water. By 1833 there were two engines, hand pumped by eight men on each side. In 1831 the Hook and Ladder Co. was formed, and the firehall was divided into three sections. The south part contained No. 1 Engine, the *York*; the centre held No.2, the *Phoenix*, and the north held the Hook and Ladder Co. In 1833, the hall housed fifty men and about 750 feet of hose.

THE ENGINE HOUSE [CENTRE] from a hand coloured photo-engraving, after a pen & ink drawing. Artist and date unrecorded. (Metropolitan Toronto Library)

PARLIAMENT BUILDINGS 1826-1892

THE LEGISLATIVE BUILDINGS STOOD IN SIMCOE PLACE, A SIX-ACRE
square bounded by Front, John, Wellington and Simcoe streets. They
faced Front Street, with a rear entrance on Wellington Street. Designed
by James Grant Chewett (1793-1862), and built by John Ewart (1788-
1856), the dignified red brick structure faced the Bay, and the
Governor's Residence occupied the block to the north. The roof was
covered with tin, in case of sparks from the chimneys. Commenced in
1826, the central block, two-storeys high and 133 feet by 90 feet, was
completed in 1830. The chambers of the Legislative Assembly on the
east side of the wide central hall, and the Legislative Council on the
west side, each with a gallery, were handsomely appointed. Two wings,
each 90 feet by 55 feet, and standing 40 feet from the centre, were
completed in 1833. During the cholera epidemic in 1834, the hospital
was so overcrowded that the lieutenant governor made the east wing of
the new buildings available for patients. Basement rooms were used as
vaults and offices, and in 1849 the spaces between the wings and centre
were filled in.

When the Parliament of Upper Canada met there in 1832, they
must have heaved a sigh of relief. Since their first meeting in 1792, they
had migrated frequently. There is a legend that the first Parliament in
Newark [Niagara-on-the-Lake], the temporary first capital, was held
under an oak tree. The first session is believed to have met in the upper
floor of the Freemasons' Hall. Others claim that Canada's first Legislature
met in Navy Hall, which the governor was using as a residence. Later
sessions in Newark were held in the additions Simcoe made to the
barracks of Butler's Rangers. He always called these "the sheds."
Simcoe returned to England in 1796, and the first Parliament in York
(proclaimed capital in 1793) was held in the new buildings, called the
"Palace of the Government", in 1797.

When the first Parliament Buildings in York were burned in 1813, the members shifted to Jordan's York Hotel for one session. They then moved into Hon. George Markland's large house at the northeast corner of Wellington and York streets. The new Parliament Buildings were ready in 1820, and they moved in, but fire again destroyed the buildings in 1824. Continuing their gypsy wanderings, the members met in the York General Hospital, the largest building in town; then in the Court House, before settling in the new Front Street buildings in 1832.

When Upper and Lower Canada were united in 1841, the members were uprooted again. They packed their books and long underwear, and headed for Kingston. Until 1867 they were like a troupe of strolling players making the circuit of Montreal in 1844, Toronto in 1849, Quebec in 1852, Toronto in 1855, Quebec in 1859 and Ottawa in 1865. During the intervals, the buildings on Front Street were used as law courts, a university, a lunatic asylum, and barracks. There was a persistent belief that they were haunted after the insane were removed. There were many reports that the ghosts of the poor lunatics were heard screaming and moaning.

In the mid 1850s, extensive additions and alterations were made by the architect William Hay. After Confederation there was much refurbishing before the Ontario Legislature could meet there. Toronto was once more a capital, and the buildings were occupied until 1892. The old structure was vacant until 1903 when it was demolished, and the Grand Trunk Railway freight sheds were built on the site. Parliament moved to Queen's Park in 1892. In the century since 1792, the Assembly had moved nearly twenty times.

PARLIAMENT BUILDINGS 1835, after a hand coloured Currier lithograph, attributed to Thomas Young, showing the four columned portico which was never built.

[52]

JOHN DOEL'S BREWERY 1827-1847

JOHN DOEL (1790-1871) FROM SOMERSET, ENGLAND, CAME TO YORK in 1818. For some years he delivered all the mail which was not called for at the post office. In 1827 he built his two-storey frame house at the northwest corner of Bay and Newgate [Adelaide] streets. In the rear he built an L-shaped frame brewery with hugh vats, which extended 100 feet up Bay Street. Doel was active in the Methodist Episcopal Church and was a member of the first City Council, 1834-35. He was also one of William Lyon Mackenzie's staunchest supporters. Because his property was on the outskirts of town, it was considered a safe place for the "Patriots" to meet. During the summer and autumn of 1837, many meetings of the more radical Reformers were held in Doel's house and in a room at the back of his brewery. Doel served on several committees.

Embittered by the conduct of the Lieutenant Governor, Sir Francis Bond Head and by their own failure to win reform by constitutional means, Mackenzie and many of his followers decided that open rebellion was now their only hope. The August 2, 1837 edition of Mackenzie's newspaper *The Constitution* contained a virtual declaration of independence. It was drawn up largely by Dr. John Rolph and Mackenzie. On November 15, the newspaper contained the draft of a proposed constitution for the "Independent State of Upper Canada". It contained more than eighty clauses and was based on separation from Great Britain. A Governor, Senate and House of Assembly were to be elected by the people. One clause stated, "The Legislature shall make no law respecting the establishment of religion or for the encouragement of any religious denomination". Crown and Clergy Reserves were to be abolished. Clause 4 prohibited any clergyman, ecclesiastic, bishop or priest from holding a seat in the Senate or Assembly, or holding any civil or military office. Justices of the Peace, Sheriffs, Coroners, Clerks of the Peace and Registrars were to be elected for each county for no longer than four years. Gold and silver were to be the only legal tender, banks were to be prohibited, and the circulation of bank notes forbidden. Militia officers, up to the rank of captain, were to be elected, and above that rank, were to be chosen by the governor on the advice of the Senate. There were many other clauses, some of which are law today.

This constitution was submitted to the meeting at Doel's Brewery on November 18, 1837, and noisy disputes broke out. Some of the cooler Reformers withdrew, and John Doel quarrelled violently with Mackenzie. Doel, Price and some others refused to take up arms against the Queen.

Following the failure of the Rebellion in the first week of December, Mackenzie escaped to Buffalo, N.Y. where he was hailed as a martyr and hero. He addressed large crowds and appealed for men and arms. With hundreds of Canadian refugees and American sympathizers, he set up a provisional government on Navy Island, a British island in the Niagara River. Recruits were attracted by his promise of three hundred acres of land when they would successfully invade the mainland. The provisional government's flag displayed two stars representing Upper and Lower Canada. The Great Seal had the twin stars and a new moon, and the words Liberty and Equality. Mackenzie printed his own money to finance the struggle. It was in the form of promissory notes in the denominations of one and ten Spanish dollars to be exchanged for cash and redeemed in four months at City Hall, Toronto. Many of these notes were made out to James Hervey Price who thus lost a great deal of money. Some of the notes were accepted by Buffalo merchants for supplies.

John Doel continued to make fine beer until 1847 when his brewery burned down.

THE DOEL RESIDENCE AND BREWERY MALT HOUSE from a pen & ink drawing in Robertson's *Landmarks of Toronto*. (Metropolitan Toronto Library)

BANK OF UPPER CANADA 1827-1861

AN ACRE OF LAND ON THE NORTH SIDE OF DUKE STREET, EAST OF George Street, had been a Crown grant for the use of a Roman Catholic Church in York. Sir William Campbell bought the land from the trustees in 1821, and sold the corner lot to the Bank of Upper Canada in 1825. The bank was the first chartered bank in the province, and had outgrown its first quarters in a converted store at the southeast corner of Frederick and King streets.

The design for the new bank has been attributed to Dr. W.W. Baldwin, but the evidence is not conclusive. It is based on a statement in *Rowsell's Toronto City Directory 1850*: "We believe the building was designed by the late Hon. Dr. W.W. Baldwin." It is true that Dr. Baldwin would have been very familiar with such splendid townhouses in his youth in Dublin. Another strong point in Baldwin's favour is the resemblance between the bank and his own 1835 house on the northeast corner of Front and Bay streets, which he did design. However, it is now known that the classic portico on the bank, so similar to the columned porch on Baldwin's house, was not added to the bank until 1843, when the architect John G. Howard added it. Evidence recently uncovered by Stephen Otto [former Executive Director of the Heritage Administration Branch, Ministry of Culture and Recreation], suggests that Francis Hall (1792-1862), may have drawn the plans for the Bank of Upper Canada. In partnership with Duncan Kennedy, Hall was the building contractor for the bank. He was also trained as a civil engineer and architect. Dr. Baldwin was a physician and lawyer, who practised architecture as a hobby, but had no formal training.

[55]

The building, the first in the province designed specifically for a bank, was of brick—the façade being of solid hewn stone. It resembled an elegant, late 18th century Georgian townhouse, with a handsome balustrade around the roof. The interior woodwork was mahogany. It was completed in 1827.

In 1851 Frederick W. Cumberland (1821-1881), designed a brick addition on the back of the bank, facing George Street, as a residence with a separate entrance for Thomas Gibbs Ridout (1792-1861), who had been cashier [general manager] since the bank's founding in 1822. With his wife Matilda, Ridout had been living on the second floor of the bank, and his quarters were required for offices. Ridout had three children by his first wife Anna Sullivan, and eleven by Matilda, who was a sister of Wilmot Bramley, architect Cumberland's wife. No doubt both the bank staff and the Ridouts were pleased when the new residence was ready. In 1861 the bank moved to Yonge Street, and the cashier died the same day.

The bank, which had granted too many loans on the security of unsaleable land, failed in 1866, and in 1870 the Christian Brothers bought the building, and added a third floor with mansard roof. They erected a three-storey building beside it, in Second Empire style, designed by Henry Langley (1836-1906), and opened the De La Salle Institute. The Roman Catholic boys' school remained there until 1913. During the war it was an R.A.F. recruiting centre, and in 1921 was bought by Christie, Brown and Company. In 1925 the United Farmers' Co-Operative Co. bought the building, using it as a storehouse until 1956. After a serious fire in 1978, the Duke Street complex was declared a National Historic Site. The buildings were bought by lawyer-historian Sheldon Godfrey and his wife Judith. The husband and wife team, after months of careful research, and at great expense, have meticulously restored the historic Bank of Upper Canada, the oldest surviving bank building in Canada. In 1981 the Godfreys were presented with a prestigious award by the Montreal firm, Credit Foncier. The old bank is now rented by DMR & Associates, and George Brown College occupies the De La Salle portion.

BANK OF UPPER CANADA from a pen & ink drawing ca 1888, attributed to W.J. Thomson, after a drawing by Sanford A. Fleming ca 1851. (Metropolitan Toronto Library)

HOME DISTRICT GRAMMAR SCHOOL 1829-1863

SECONDARY SCHOOLS WERE CALLED GRAMMAR SCHOOLS UNTIL 1871, and the first public school in York was not an elementary school, but the Home District Grammar School. It opened in 1807, in one room attached to the Reverend George O'Kill Stuart's home. There were five pupils (boys) who paid fees, but Stuart, the schoolmaster, was no more successful at teaching than he was as minister of the Anglican Church, where his sing song delivery drove one parishioner to leave whenever he began to preach. In 1812 Dr. John Strachan succeeded as headmaster and rector. His school was held in a rented barn at King and Yonge streets. The General Quarter Sessions granted £400 in 1816 for a school, which was erected in the six acre College Square north of St. James' Church. It was a two-storey frame building facing Church Street, which was painted blue after Strachan raised the money by giving a series of public lectures. The Blue School was 55 feet by 40 feet and held about fifty pupils. Unpainted pine desks faced the long north and south walls of the ground floor room. The upstairs had a platform at the east end, and on public days parents and officials came to hear debates and recitations. Dr. Strachan was a "born" teacher; enrolment increased and assistants were needed. Various young men, some studying for holy orders under Strachan and living with him, were junior masters. In 1824 Strachan retired from teaching and went on to a distinguished career in the church and government, becoming the first Anglican bishop in Upper Canada in 1839. His successor was Samuel Armour, a Glasgow graduate. In 1825 Rev. Thomas Phillips, a Cambridge man, became headmaster. He wore antique clerical clothes with shovel hat, and

[57]

powdered his hair, except when in mourning. He introduced texts used at Eton—the Greek Grammar having explanations and vocabulary solely in Latin. George A. Barber came with him as assistant and introduced a form of cricket.

When Upper Canada College was founded in 1829, the Blue School was moved to the southeast corner of Jarvis and Lombard streets. While the College's buildings were being erected in Russell Square, north of Government House, the two schools were amalgamated under the name of Upper Canada College and Royal Grammar School. The old school was refurbished and a one-storey addition built. When Upper Canada College's buildings were ready, the combined school moved to the new location leaving the Blue School vacant. The union was stormy; there was controversy over curriculum and ownership of the original site, and in 1834 the Grammar School returned to its old building. It remained there until 1864, when it moved to Dalhousie Street, north of Gould, and admitted girls. The old Blue School was degraded to a junk yard and was demolished in the early 1870s. In 1869 the trustees bought a site on Jarvis Street, south of Carlton Street, and William Kauffman designed the building named Toronto High School (opened in 1871), which was changed to Jarvis Street Collegiate Institute in 1890. The school on the present site, at the southeast corner of Jarvis and Wellesley streets, was opened in 1924.

The old Grammar School became the Toronto Grammar School, Toronto High School, Toronto Collegiate, and is now Jarvis Collegiate Institute.

HOME DISTRICT GRAMMAR SCHOOL from a watercolour and ink, artist and date unknown. (Metropolitan Toronto Library)

OSGOODE HALL 1829

THE ORIGINAL BUILDING, NOW THE EAST WING, WAS DESIGNED BY the master builder, John Ewart, as a home for the Law Society of Upper Canada, which was incorporated in 1797. Six acres of land were bought from Attorney General John Beverley Robinson in 1828 for £1000, and construction was begun the following year under the careful eye of Dr. W.W. Baldwin, Treasurer of the Society. It was a square, red brick building, two-and-a-half storeys high, minus the modern portico and was called Osgoode Hall in honour of William Osgoode, the first Chief Justice of Upper Canada. It was on the north side of Lot [Queen] Street, facing down York Street and quite remote from York proper.

There was no law school yet. Students articled for five years under a barrister and were then examined orally by the Benchers [governors] of the Law Society. Barristers and students could live in the attic of the Hall, but the Society found that it lost money because of unpaid bills for board, beer and candles. During the Rebellion of 1837, the government took over the building as a barracks, and soldiers remained there for the next seven years. The scarlet coat and tartan kilt were in great contrast to black legal gowns, and everyone enjoyed the lively music provided by bands in front of the Hall every afternoon.

In 1844 a similar west wing was erected for high courts, and both wings were given a classical stone portico and were connected by an arcaded centre with a small dome. The architect was Henry Bower Lane. In 1855 the first lecturers to the students were appointed, but the law school was not established until 1872.

A complete renovation by Cumberland and Storm was begun in 1857 which removed the dome, created the present south façade and added more court rooms. The classic iron fence with its baffle gates was erected at the same time. These were designed with narrow openings to keep out wandering cows, but also gave trouble to portly legal figures. All was completed in nice time for the gala reception of H.R.H. Edward, prince of Wales in 1860. The magnificent Great Library became a ballroom for the occasion, which was the social event of the year.

In 1968 the law school moved to York University and its building was taken over by the Bar Admission Course. The last great celebration was in 1973 and H.M. Queen Mother Elizabeth re-opened the building. Historic Osgoode Hall has dual ownership and dual functions: as seat of the Superior Courts of Ontario, part of it is owned by the province. The Law Society still owns the east wing with its fine wood panelling and plaster mouldings, and part of the centre.

Extensive searches by both legal and architectural researchers have failed to turn up a sketch of the original Osgoode Hall. However, the first building stands as the east wing of the present edifice. We can therefore obtain a clear view of the structure as it appeared in 1834 by visually masking out the centre and west sections and removing the modern columned portico and handsome iron fence.

OSGOODE HALL from a stero taken from the southeast ca 1870. (Archives of Ontario)

YORK GENERAL HOSPITAL 1829-1856

DURING THE WAR OF 1812 THE ONLY CHURCH (ST. JAMES') WAS converted into a hospital and in 1817 it was realized that a civilian hospital was needed. A Board of Trustees was appointed and the first money raised largely in England was provided by the Loyal and Patriotic Society organized in 1812, which had ordered medals (gold, silver, bronze) for those who had served with merit. There was great difficulty in deciding who should be awarded. Thus the medals were never presented, but were melted down. From the bullion and other funds the Society presented £4000 to the Trustees for the construction of a hospital which was begun in 1820. A two-storey red brick building, 107 feet by 66 feet, and in Georgian style, was erected at the southeast corner of the block bounded by King, Adelaide, John and Peter streets. The building was not finished in 1824 when the Parliament Buildings burned down. The government took over the hospital and hastily completed it and the Legislature sat there until Sir John Colborne restored it to the hospital. The York General Hospital with fifty beds was opened in June 1829 and the Legislature voted it an annual grant. Dr. Christopher Widmer (1870-1858), an ex-army surgeon, and a member of the Upper Canadian Medical Board from 1819 until his death, took a leading part in the founding and early development of the hospital. It was intended only for the deserving poor. Those who could, paid a shilling a day, but if destitute were given free care. During the serious cholera epidemic in 1832, John Ritchie's tender of £50 was accepted, and two small isolation buildings, called Pest Houses, were added in the rear. Dr. Isaac Stephenson was the resident physician at the time. By 1834 there were fifteen licensed doctors in town and the hospital changed its name to the Toronto General Hospital. By 1853 it was quite inadequate and a new hospital was begun on Gerrard Street which opened in 1856. The old building was used for government offices for three years, then was empty until 1862 when it was demolished. The Arlington Hotel later occupied the site.

YORK GENERAL HOSPITAL from a watercolour attributed to F.V. Poole ca 1912. (Metropolitan Toronto Library)

THE CUSTOMS HOUSE 1829-1835

IN 1829 GEORGE SAVAGE, A JEWELLER AND WATCHMAKER WITH A business on King Street, became Collector of Customs. He established a customs house, the fourth in York, in temporary quarters in Isaac Columbus' shop, fronting on Duke Street. In 1829 he removed the customs offices to the one-and-a-half storey brick cottage of Thomas Carfrae on the east side of Scott Street, near Wellington Street. Carfrae and his family occupied the south end of the building and the customs office occupied the north half. Though Savage was known for his vigilance, smugglers occasionally tricked him into following false leads while the contraband escaped him. One of the most daring smugglers was Michael Masterson, whose cottage was on the shore at the foot of Bay Street. He was called "Fisty" Masterson because he wore a hook in place of a lost hand. Fisty was very handy with his hook and frequently outwitted both Savage and Carfrae, who succeeded Savage when he died in 1835.

FOURTH CUSTOMS HOUSE (an 1834 view) from a pen & ink appearing in Robertson's *Landmarks of Toronto.* (Metropolitan Toronto Library)

YORK HOUSE 1831-1905

HON. CHRISTOPHER ALEXANDER HAGERMAN (1792-1847), ATTORNEY General of Upper Canada, built a large brick house at the northeast corner of Wellington and Graves [Simcoe] streets, across from Government House. He added a two-storey building to the north, on Simcoe Street, for his office. Considered a mansion, it had a handsome front door and interior walnut panelling. The drawing room, panelled in white woodwork was located upstairs. The 1831 Mary O'Brien Journal said it was "well appointed in genteel style." Stable and coach house were behind a high fence. Hagerman became a judge in 1840. The house was bought in 1847 by John W. Crawford, who moved to Government House in 1873 when he became lieutenant governor. The Ontario government then bought York House, using the house as attorney general's offices and the annex as an immigration bureau. When the government moved to Queen's Park in 1892, York House was vacated. It became a boarding house and was demolished in 1905.

YORK HOUSE (showing Hagerman's law office to the left) from a watercolour attributed to F.V. Poole ca 1912, after a pen & ink ca 1888. (Metropolitan Toronto Library)

[64]

ST. JAMES' CHURCH 1831-1839

THE CONGREGATION OF THE FIRST WOODEN CHURCH ON THE
north side of King Street, east of Church Street, had grown so great that
a larger building was needed. The cornerstone was laid in June 1832 and
the church was finished in 1833, except for the tower. James Grant
Chewett, son of William Chewett, who was Deputy Surveyor General
and a member of the congregation, was clerk of the works, and is
credited with the austere Greek design. John Ritchey was the builder.

Built of Kingston limestone, the exterior dimensions were 149 feet
by 80 feet and the church could seat three thousand people. The pews,
chancel panelling, and fronts of the galleries, built by John Lacey the
joiner, were of fine, carved black walnut. A sum of £7425 was voted to
pay the cost. The old church was sold for £62 and demolished. The
pulpit, reading desk, communion rails and some of the square pews
were given to a church in Scarborough.

The celebrated author and art critic, Anna Jameson, whose domestic
disappointments soured her observations when she visited Toronto in
1836 and 1837, wrote in her *Winter Studies and Summer Rambles in Canada*
"... one very ugly church without tower or steeple ... government
offices built of staring red brick in the most tasteless and vulgar style
imaginable". On another occasion she wrote, "The interior of the
Episcopal Church here is rather elegant, with the exception of a huge
window of painted glass which cost £500 and is in vile, tawdry taste."

[65]

In January 1839 the "exceedingly beautiful Church", as Dr. Strachan described it, was partially destroyed by fire. Only the walls remained. The loss of the recently installed organ was a bitter blow. The proposed tower and bells had not yet been added.

ST. JAMES' CHURCH from a pen & ink appearing in Robertson's, *Landmarks of Toronto.* (Metropolitan Toronto Library)

FREELAND'S SOAP FACTORY 1832

ONE OF THE FIRST MANUFACTURING ESTABLISHMENTS IN YORK WAS Freeland's Soap and Candle Factory, located on the lakefront on the east side of the Yonge Street Wharf. Brothers Peter and William Freeland came to York from Glasgow in 1830 and erected a building 90 feet long, 40 feet wide, and three-storeys high. It was built on cribs 12 feet in the water. They imported large iron kettles from Scotland and candle moulds from the U.S.A. The sheds in the centre and on the right stored wood ashes, lime and ice. The shed on the left stored barrels of rendered tallow, brought in schooners from Rochester. Canadian and Russian tallow was also used. Palm oil from Africa was also stored there. The buildings in the rear were built in 1841 on the Yonge Street Wharf. Eventually Peter owned the whole wharf, henceforth called Freeland's Wharf. His son Robert invented soap making machinery.

FREELAND'S SOAP & CANDLE FACTORY from a watercolour attributed to F.V. Poole ca 1912, after a pen & ink ca 1888. (Metropolitan Toronto Library)

THE TOWN HALL 1833-1844

THE TOWN HALL SHARED SPACE WITH THE SECOND MARKET BUILDING, on the south side of King Street, west of New Street [Jarvis]. The old wooden market building was replaced by a quadrangular brick structure, which was designed by James Grant Chewett (1792-1862), and Dr. W.W. Baldwin (1774-1844). There were arched entrances with gates in the four sides, and the perimeter of Market Square was marked with posts and an iron chain. The building was authorized by the magistrates sitting in Quarter Sessions, and was completed in 1833. They borrowed money by issuing debentures of £6000 but the building cost £9240 when completed, and this huge debt was one of the arguments for incorporation. A wooden gallery ran around the four sides above the stalls of butchers, farmers and grocers. A noisy demonstration in the gallery in 1834 against increased taxes caused the gallery to collapse, and a number of men were horribly injured on the butchers' upturned hooks; several were killed. At the front of the building over the King Street entrance, was a large room (holding one hundred) used by the town officials, and on occasion was used for concerts and public meetings.

In March 1834 the Town Hall became Toronto's first City Hall, and continued to share the building with the market until 1844, when the new City Hall on Front Street was opened. The King Street building housed the market until the Great Fire of 1849. The front of the building was so severely damaged that the whole market had to be demolished.

THE TOWN HALL from a pen & ink attributed to Owen Staples ca 1912, after a drawing by Henry Scadding ca 1888. (Metropolitan Toronto Library)

[68]

BLACK BULL & DROVERS' ARMS 1833

THE OLD INN AT THE NORTHEAST CORNER OF QUEEN AND MARIA streets was a frame building, with a swinging sign and a wooden horse trough and pump in front. The Black Bull was a favourite stopping spot for farmers coming to York from the north and west. Maria Willcocks and her sister Phoebe [Mrs. W.W. Baldwin] owned the 100 acre lot running up to modern Bloor Street, and rented the farm to Mossop, who built the inn and was the first landlord. The sisters sold part of the lot to Joseph Leuty, who opened up Maria and Phoebe Streets. Maria was later renamed Soho Street. In 1834 the proprietor of the Black Bull was J. Butcher Baker. The inn was later rebuilt in brick and eventually became the Clifton Hotel.

BLACK BULL & DROVERS' ARMS from a watercolour attributed to Owen Staples ca 1912 after a pen and ink by C.W. Jefferys ca 1888. (Metropolitan Toronto Library)

THE POST OFFICE 1833-1838

JAMES SCOTT HOWARD (1798-1866), WAS BORN IN IRELAND, CAME TO York in 1820 and became postmaster in 1828. At that time the postmaster had to provide the building, in which he and his family lived, and pay for staff, fuel, candles and stationery. In April 1833 Howard bought 60 feet of land from the Bank of Upper Canada, which occupied the northeast corner of Duke and George streets. The lot was east of the bank, with a vacant lot between, and was west of Chief Justice Campbell's house. Howard built a three-storey red brick Georgian style house for himself, which would house the post office in the west end, with a separate entrance. The contractor was John Richards, whose agreement lists "cubberts in the kitchen [basement] and nine and a half days work at the poast office". Alex Hamilton did the painting, papering and glazing, the sanding of four fireplaces, and the cutting and gilding of letters for the post office sign. The post office was listed in the 1833 Directory as open. When York became Toronto the next year, it was the city's first and only post office. During the Rebellion of 1837 Howard was unjustly accused of disloyalty, and was dismissed in 1838. He sold the building to Huson [Hudson] Murray, who lived there for many years. T.D. Harris then occupied it until 1874, when the Christian Brothers bought it for their De La Salle Institute. Windows and roof line were altered to harmonize with the other mansard type school buildings, and Howard's house and post office were forgotten. In 1925 the school buildings were forgotten. In 1925 the school buildings were bought by the United Farmers' Co-Operative

Co. Ltd. Windows were bricked in and the building became a cold storage plant. When the complex was sold in 1956, the structure began to decay. It was empty for some years while waiting for demolition, and nearly burned down. A rescue project headed by Sheldon Godfrey, M.A.,LL.B. and his wife Judith began the difficult task of restoring the building. In her careful research of records Judith made the important discovery that it was Toronto's first post office, and is believed to be not only a relic of York, but the oldest surviving post office in Canada.

JAMES SCOTT HOWARD HOUSE (post office) from a watercolour attributed to Owen Staples ca 1912, after a drawing by Owen Staples ca 1888. (Metropolitan Toronto Library)

THE BRITISH COFFEE HOUSE 1833-1855

THE SOUTHEAST CORNER OF YORK AND KING STREETS WAS GRANTED to Deputy Surveyor William Chewett in 1805. In 1833 John G. Howard, architect, designed Chewett's Buildings, York's first office block, for William's son, James G. Chewett. John Cotter's British Coffee House occupied the corner of the building with its entrance on York Street. Members of parliament and the elite stayed there, room and board costing $1.00 a day. A visitor to York in 1832 wrote, "We were well accommodated at the British Coffee House, good cokery [sic], very middling ale and vile table beer". There were about ten stores on the King Street side, with dwellings above. Howard had his office and living quarters there until 1837. The government suspected that rebels were meeting in the Coffee House and closed it in 1837. During the Rebellion and until 1842, it was used as a barracks. It then became Ellah's a private hotel with the Toronto Club renting quarters. In 1852, a dancing academy rented part of the hotel and held popular balls. The Rossin Brothers bought the land and building in 1855, demolished it and erected the Rossin House.

BRITISH COFFEE HOUSE from a pen & ink attributed to Owen Staples ca 1889, after a watercolour by John G. Howard (date unrecorded). (Metropolitan Toronto Library)

[72]

THE THEATRE ROYAL 1834

THE FIRST METHODIST CONGREGATION IN YORK WAS A GROUP OF
Episcopal Methodists under the American Conference, who founded a
chapel in 1818, served by circuit missionaries from the U.S.A., who
tended to preach the benefits of republicanism. The loyal element,
called the British Wesleyans, with ministers from England, left and
built their own meeting house on the east side of George Street, south
of Queen Street. The chapel of the original group, built by Mr. Robert
Petch on the south side of King Street, west of York, was a frame
building 60 feet by 40 feet. The gable end facing King Street had two
doors, the east one for women who sat on that side, and the west one for
men who sat on the west side. When the Methodists moved to a larger
brick church on Adelaide Street in 1833, the frame chapel was bought
by the American John Waugh, a sign painter, who managed the Red
Lion Hotel on Market Lane, and his brother Samuel, a professional
artist. They painted the interior to resemble an ancient cathedral and
fitted it up as a place of amusement called the Theatre Royal. Their first
exhibition was a panorama, "The Burning of Moscow," which by an
ingenious contrivance, kept the flames in constant motion devouring
the city with terrifying realism. This popular entertainment was shown
for many months. Another attraction was the Chinese Kaleidoscope,
which gave the appearance of a large fireworks display. Comic songs,
dances and recitations were provided by Irish American theatrical
groups, who followed the circuit around the Great Lakes.

THE THEATRE ROYAL from a watercolour attributed to John Cotton ca 1912.
(Metropolitan Toronto Library)

[73]

INDEX

PRINTED
FOR
THE PAGET PRESS
IN
NOVEMBER 1983
DESIGN
&
TYPOGRAPHY
BY
EILDON GRAPHICA